How Leaders Can Strengthen Their Organization's Culture

28 Simple and Effective Ways

Tim Burningham

A *TAB* Original
Houston, Texas

PO BOX 5156
Houston, TX 77325

Distributed by The Awesome Boss LLC

For ordering information or special discounts for bulk purchases, please contact The Awesome Boss LLC at PO Box 5156, Houston, TX, 77325, or, betheawesomeboss@gmail.com.

Library of Congress Cataloging-In-Publication Data

Burningham, Tim.

Leader's Strengthen Organization's Culture: 28 simple and effective ways/ Tim Burningham, 2nd ed.
p. ; cm.

Issued also as an ebook

ISBN: 9781793928498

1.   Leadership effectiveness. 2. Organizational culture 3. Business I. Title

Printed in the United States of America

Second Edition

TAB 23 22 21 31 05 11 12

The Center for Company Culture

Additional help and resources can be found at

TheCenterforCompanyCulture.com

BeAnAwesomeBoss.com

TheCenterforCompanyCulture.thinkific.com

Also by Tim Burningham

Be An Awesome Boss!: The Four C's Model to Leadership Success

Preface

Throughout my career I've had the privilege of leading several diverse teams in many different states across the country as a department director, executive, corporate director, president, and CEO. During this time I've worked closely with countless leaders as their co-worker, partner, colleague, boss, resource, coach, mentor, and friend.

During my experience, I've observed that many leaders are not as interested or committed as they should be to the simple (and often free) things that make a work environment great. When asked, most leaders will state they want a strong culture that attracts the best talent and ultimately produces good results, but they often don't understand or at least embrace what they ought to do to build such a culture.

Unfortunately, many leaders gravitate toward elaborate programs or big events almost as a way to prove they are dedicated to creating an award-winning culture. To illustrate this point, let me share an example.

In 2005, I was working for a large hospital in Texas that, on a quarterly basis, gave away *a brand-new car* to a lucky employee. This fortunate staff member was someone who qualified to have their name entered into the car giveaway drawing based on their supervisor's recommendation of their performance.

It was exciting for a few moments during the big giveaway announcement—in fact, it was hard to believe it was really happening!

After the name of the winner was called, the enthusiasm and anticipation of the moment quickly wore off, and soon everyone was back to business as usual. This unbelievable employee appreciation program did little to change performance or results.

I recall sitting in a leadership team meeting while the executives wondered why their people still weren't happy—they were giving away _free cars_, for heaven's sake! As you might guess, this program soon faded away.

What I learned by observing this and many other similar programs throughout my career is that elaborate giveaways or super hyped-up employee appreciation programs don't seem to work. They always fall flat when enacted in isolation. Alone, these programs are not enough to build a strong culture.

In this hospital's situation, the truth was the leaders weren't committed to doing the little things to show appreciation and help people feel valued each day—thus, their results didn't improve.

So how do you change a culture and strengthen it to help your organization? How do you increase productivity and engagement among your team while lessening workplace politics, drama, confusion, and turnover?

As the old adage goes, "People don't care how much you know until they know how much you care." Often, the simple things leaders consistently do mean the most to their people. Simple, consistent acts are the most powerful force in creating a culture that leads to improved performance and superior results.

If nothing else, this knowledge should be incredibly empowering to all leaders. The fact is, anyone can apply these simple ideas to improve the strength of their organization's culture. It doesn't depend on a high-level degree from a prestigious university or years and years of experience. It doesn't require the financial means to hold a quarterly car giveaway or the sophistication to do intricate data analysis. Anyone in any organization can be a great leader and create an amazing culture that engages a team and produces results. Anyone, anywhere, can significantly improve the strength of their company's culture through small and simple actions.

Contents

Introduction

Nothing is more important in today's competitive work environment than the strength of an organization's culture.

Culture is the shared beliefs, assumptions, behaviors, and norms that exist within an organization. It is both the written and unwritten rules people live by. A company's culture is fluid, not static.

A strong culture is one where minimal politics and confusion exist, turnover is low among good employees, engagement and productivity are high, and results are consistently good.

Leaders must find ways to strengthen the culture within their organizations. Those who do will be rewarded not only with greater success, but also greater fulfillment at work.

This book offers leaders—supervisors, department heads, team leads, managers, directors, vice presidents, executives, CEOs—simple and effective ways to impact the culture of the teams they lead.

Why are the ideas in this book simple?

One of my favorite authors, Stephen R. Covey, often talked about the impact a trim tab has on a large ship. Though the trim tab itself is a simple and very small mechanism, it has the power to change the entire direction of an enormous vessel.

If you looked at a trim tab alone, you might not think much of it—it would be easy to overlook its potential and value. However, this wouldn't change its capacity, when utilized, to impact the course of the ship.

The suggestions offered in this book are like a trim tab—small and simple. Many can be done with minimal effort. Most may not seem astounding or significant at first glance. But, like the trim tab on a boat, they contain within them the ability to have an enormous impact on the direction of your organization. Don't let the simplicity of the ideas in this book distract you from their potential.

Likewise, just as many of these actions are easy to take, they are also easy to ignore, undervalue, and forget. It takes discipline and a certain belief in their inherent value to consistently do them.

When implemented, the ideas in this book will help you "trim tab" your way to a strong organizational culture. Within time, practicing these ideas can produce wildly different results—better results—results and fulfillment you've never imagined possible in your organization.

The bottom line is small and simple things work in helping leaders create strong cultures!

Three precautionary warnings

Here are three precautionary heads-ups that you should know as you begin this book:

Heads-up #1

Most of the ideas in this book you've probably heard before. Rather than provide groundbreaking insights, this book's purpose is to serve as a reminder of the power that comes from doing simple things consistently over time. With that being said, I'm sure there will be at least one or two ideas that may be new to you.

Heads-up #2

Many of the ideas, if implemented only halfway or without consistency, may unintentionally hurt your culture more than help it. For example, suggestion #6 is to hand out birthday cards. If you deliver cards to everyone with a birthday in January but forget to do it in February and March, then start up again in April and May, then stop in June, you might imagine how some of your team members may be bothered by the fact that their peers received birthday cards from you while they didn't. So, be sure you are 100 percent committed to an idea before choosing to implement it. Have the resolve to stay consistent and disciplined in carrying out the concept; otherwise, don't do it.

Heads-up #3

Don't feel overwhelmed by the number of suggestions in this book. You do not need to do all 28 to have success. The reality is that consistently implementing just one of these ideas will have a tremendous impact on strengthening your culture. So, take it one step at a time. Start with one or two actions and focus on them until they become a habit. Then move on to more.

With that out of the way, let's get on with the 28 simple and effective ways leaders can strengthen their culture!

*Names used in the stories throughout the book have been changed.

#1

Simplify and Share (Often) Your Mission Statement

At the heart of a good organizational culture is helping people understand *the why* of the work they do. When building a strong culture, this is the best place to start.

A mission statement should provide a clear unifying purpose that is shared throughout the entire organization or team that you lead.

We all yearn for purpose. It's part of our human fiber. We all want to make a contribution to something bigger than ourselves. We want to know that what we do matters.

When companies don't define their purpose, the odds of living up to their purpose drastically decrease. And when there is no purpose at work, or when the purpose isn't clear, work can become unsatisfying and even feel pointless.

Many leaders try to motivate their teams by lighting a fire underneath their people—but this type of motivation rarely lasts. Providing a clear purpose, however, will light a fire *within* your people that can motivate them forever.

Too many mission statements don't help people know why the organization does what it does. Many are too long and hard to understand. When this is the case, the mission nearly always ends up becoming nothing more than words on a piece of paper.

To help people understand and work toward a purpose, a mission statement must be simple. This means it ought to be straightforward, concise, and easy to remember. A well-crafted mission statement that will have a big impact on culture should be no more than one or two sentences long.

Once a mission statement is well-written, it should be repeated by the organization's leaders frequently. It should also influence decisions and become a significant part of each system and process that involves your people, such as the interview, onboarding, new employee orientation, and employee evaluation processes, for example.

You can't share your mission statement too often. The goal of every leader should be to repeat it enough (in different forms of communication) that the majority of those they lead know it and nearly have it memorized. When people can repeat the mission statement, you know you are on the right track. Thus, repetition by a leader is crucial!

Story

One health care center I worked with had a very long and confusing mission statement; however, the leadership team had a practice of repeating it together during their daily morning meeting. I had to applaud them for their efforts, but when I asked them individually what the mission statement truly meant to them and the purpose behind their work every day, it resulted in a large assortment of different answers and confusion.

While working with this team, we were able to break down and rework their mission statement into something that was simple, easy to repeat and understand, and also inspiring to them.

Their simplified mission statement was: "Our mission is to help each person we serve feel we truly care about them." That was it!

These 15 words gave the team a clear purpose. They were on a mission each day to show they cared about those they served. That was the point of their work.

This team was instantly motivated by their simplified and clear mission statement, and everyone in the organization knew exactly why they came to work each day.

Now, what if you are a leader of a small team or department within a larger organization? How do you craft a meaningful mission statement when you can't really change the mission of the entire company?

If your organization's mission statement is not helpful and you don't have the power to change or improve it, create a new one for your team or your department. Having your own clear reason *why* you and your team do what you do every day will help you build the kind of culture within your team that will produce results.

Story

As a department director at a large hospital on the East Coast, my team and I created our own purpose-filled mission statement that guided *the why* behind what we did.

Though other departments in the hospital didn't share the mission statement we created, it gave our team clarity, purpose, and motivation to perform and exceed expectations each day.

After introducing and clarifying our mission, within time, our department's results began to greatly improve. Soon, other leaders at the hospital were asking what we were doing differently to achieve

our much-improved results. It all started
with establishing a clear purpose.

If you are struggling to simplify your mission statement,
you are not alone. To help, the question you need to ask
yourself is: "Why do I and my team come to work every
day at our organization?" Answer that question as
succinctly as you can, and you'll have the beginnings of a
great mission statement.

When simplified and shared often, a mission statement is
an extremely powerful force toward creating a strong
organizational culture.

#2

Define Your Core Values

Very often organizations have core values, but many times they aren't well-defined. Different words mean different things to different people, so simply throwing out words as values isn't good enough—or at least they won't help you strengthen your culture like they should.

Defining your core values in simple terms will help people understand what they mean and what is truly valued at work. It will give them knowledge about what the company is striving to embody and what behaviors will help them be most successful.

Story

When I was a leader at a health care center, we had the core value of "family." In essence, we wanted our team members to feel they belonged to an organization that cared about them, and we wanted them to care for one another. We also hoped the "family" value would encourage our team to provide care to our patients as if they were taking care of their own mother, son, or grandfather.

18

We mentioned our value of "family" from time to time, but it was never very well-defined. Most of us in leadership assumed "family" was a positive, loving, noncomplicated word and that everyone on our team was on the same page when we spoke about it.

I soon learned, however, that a few of our staff members were confused and often joked about what our core value of "family" implied.

Upon gaining further insight, I learned that a portion of our employees had experienced or were experiencing very difficult family situations. Many had been mistreated, taken advantage of, or abused by family members. Thus, "family" carried a much different meaning to them than what the organization intended.

Clearly defining all of our core values helped everyone on our team understand how we wanted to behave and treat others. The simple word "family," until we defined it, did not communicate clearly to all of our staff the level of care and concern we hoped to have within our organization.

If you are skeptical about this, ask some people on your team to define a core value of your organization and see what happens.

Story

> While working with a team who had a core value of "integrity," I asked different leaders to define what the value meant to them and their company. The CEO was surprised by what was shared.
>
> This simple exercise revealed a clear disconnect between what the organization hoped "integrity" would mean to their people and what it actually meant to them.

Defining values is as simple as attaching a few quick bullets points to each of them. Doing this clarifies the behaviors you expect your people to exude.

Values properly used in an organization have the greatest power in changing behavior. When people clearly understand what you hope they will represent, they will respond—and your culture will be strengthened.

If you're a manager or department leader in an organization where core values aren't clear or well-defined, you should define them for the team you lead. Tell them what the core values mean to you and why you believe they are important. Don't allow your team to speculate about their meaning or even make their own best assumptions. Make it very clear what you and your department stand for.

Once defined, much like your mission statement, the values must be repeated often. Likewise, they should influence decisions and become a core component in all the systems and processes that involve people, such as the interview process and new employee orientation.

A good leader who wants to strengthen their company's culture will repeat the well-defined core values of their organization often and do all they can to live up to them.

#3

Be an Example

I debated back and forth about whether I should include this one in the book. "Be an example" seems so obvious, yet the number of leaders I've observed who regularly exhibit behavioral misalignment is surprising.

Behavioral misalignment is acting in ways contrary to what you establish as your mission and core values. It's also saying and expecting one thing but then doing another.

Nothing undermines a leader's ability to influence a team more than behavioral misalignment.

I believe this is all too common for two primary reasons.

First, it is simply hard to always be a good example. Like everyone, leaders are humans with weaknesses and thus struggle to live up to established ideals. However, if leaders are genuine and sincere in striving to live up to what they profess, people will take notice and will cut them slack. Nevertheless, that slack is not limitless and will run out if behavioral misalignment is constant—even despite good intentions. For this reason, it is important for leaders to work hard to align themselves with the values, expectations, and culture they hope to establish.

Second, leaders undervalue the impact their example has on others and therefore fail to set a clear model of the

22

behavioral expectations they preach. This includes leaders who believe (or pretend to believe) they are just like everyone else in the organization, and therefore their words and actions carry as much clout as anyone else's.

If you are leading people, then you must accept the fact that your actions, words, and behaviors speak very loudly. They communicate a strong message to those you lead—whether you choose to believe it or not. Your people are watching your every move and will frequently overanalyze and read into your every word and action. Don't assume those you lead aren't watching, listening, or paying attention—because they always are. And don't assume they won't follow your example, because, often in unexpected ways, they will.

Story

I once worked with an executive who chose to miss a lot of work. He had a good team that would cover for him, but his people noticed he was often gone.

This leader's behavior slowly led others to believe that choosing to consistently miss work was OK. They figured their team would continue to perform well in their absence.

As you might guess, the culture of the department slowly eroded and results suffered—so much so that within time, the executive leading the department was replaced.

Conversely, I once worked with a leader who took over a health care center that was really struggling. This particular center was among the worst performers in the entire organization at that time, and its leaders had what seemed to be valid excuses for the center's lack of performance. They shared these excuses often with others, and most in the organization accepted them and believed the center would never perform well.

When this new leader arrived, she heard her team's excuses; however, she refused to adopt them as her own. She showed a determination and belief that the center could not only overcome its challenges but could also become a top performer.

As a result of her unwavering faith, I watched how each leader who worked under her slowly dropped their longstanding excuses and began to believe they could conquer their challenges as well.

Within time, this team was consistently achieving stellar results and became a top performer in the entire organization.

As a leader, your personal example provides a tremendous force in establishing the right culture. John Wooden, the legendary UCLA basketball coach who won 10 NCAA championships in 12 seasons in the 1960s and 70s, said, "Your most powerful tool [as a leader] is your own example."

If you lead others, fully accepting this simple truth offered by Coach Wooden will change and improve your culture (and possibly even change and improve you!).

Living in a way that demonstrates the type of culture you want to have can be a game changer for any organization. Company culture in many ways starts with the example set by the leader at the top.

#4

Learn Names

Few things are more pleasant to hear than the sound of someone calling you by name, and it's incredibly important to feel known at work, especially by your leader! It might take some extra work and effort on your part, but learning the names of those you work with can have a big impact on your culture.

Story

As a young CEO at a health care center, I walked into a very difficult situation with a team who had been struggling for a while. Employee turnover was high, and the staff was distrustful of leaders. It was also a challenge to recruit new employees, and much of the care being provided was done by contracted workers.

While embracing the new challenge, the first thing I decided to do was learn everyone's name that I possibly could. For some reason, this became my number one priority.

Within a short amount of time, I knew nearly every employee's name and always addressed them by name whenever I saw them. To my surprise, after a short while, the atmosphere within the center had changed.

By simply knowing and calling people by their name, I could tell they suddenly felt cared about and known. They also began to believe they were an important and valued member of our team.

As nice as it is for an individual to hear their own name, what this simple practice does for a leader is even more important. When leaders make an effort to get to know their team members, something inside of them changes and their perspective about work shifts.

Rather than viewing a staff member simply as someone to manage, the employee becomes a person to learn more about and build a relationship with. And when a leader knows their team members on more than just a superficial level, amazing things begin to happen for that company's culture.

Learning the names of the people in your organization will change how you view those you lead and will invite you to deepen your relationship with them.

Leaders who learn their team members' names show up differently at work and improve their own performance as leaders. And this, in turn, enhances the performance of those they lead.

Depending on the size of your organization, it may be hard to learn everyone's name, but make a true effort to know as many as you can—including those one, two, or even many levels below you.

If you can make it your goal to never walk by someone in your organization without looking them in the eye and greeting them by their name, you will dramatically improve your culture.

#5

Align Your People Systems with Your Mission and Values

It will probably be helpful if we begin with a definition. People systems are all the processes in your organization that involve your people. These include interviewing, onboarding, new employee orientation, employee training, rewards and recognition programs, compensation, employee evaluation, and disciplinary processes. Organizations with strong cultures ensure these important people systems focus on reinforcing the mission and values of the company.

Aligning your people systems with your company's mission and values creates incredible clarity around what matters most. It also communicates a strong message to your people that you are serious about the purpose (mission) and behavioral expectations (values) of the organization.

Story

As CEO of a health care center, my colleagues and I knew that if we wanted a strong culture, we needed to align our people systems around our mission, vision, and values. Though it took some

29

time to redesign our people systems, we eventually got there. We even went so far as to revamp our employment application. In it, we included a section that was all about our culture. It asked applicants to respond to a few important questions about how they represented our core values and how they would go about living our mission.

Regardless if they were applying for a physician or housekeeping position, no applicant could move on to the interview process without first completing this vital section of the employment application.

Studies have shown it takes at least seven times for someone to hear something before they understand it, internalize it, and believe it. I've found as a leader that the number seven is sometimes too low.

Given the number of new programs, initiatives, and policies leaders roll out and then forget about, it's no wonder that employees are often skeptical of mission statements or values. Rarely do they actually stick. However, weaving the mission and values throughout all of an organization's people systems provides constant reminders to staff that the mission and values matter. And if this idea is implemented effectively, employees will have heard about them at least seven times within their first few weeks of employment.

Establishing organizational clarity around what matters most to an organization is critical to creating a strong culture.

#6

Give Personalized Birthday Cards

Writing personal birthday cards is an extremely effective way to communicate to your team that you know them and value them. Though it is a very simple action, not enough leaders discipline themselves to do it on a consistent basis.

One reason for this, I believe, is because leaders worry that some of their team members will barely glance at the card when they receive it. The idea of spending time to write and deliver a card only to have it immediately disposed of is discouraging. Thus, leaders justify avoiding this task by telling themselves it won't mean all that much to their team.

Though a few members of your team may seem unimpressed when receiving a birthday card from you, this shouldn't keep you from doing it. Because for many others, it will mean the world to them.

Story

When I was the CEO at a health care center, I delivered a birthday card to a third-shift certified nursing assistant (CNA) at 4:30 a.m. (For those not familiar with health care, third shift is the overnight shift that is often overlooked.) When I handed her the card and said "Happy birthday!" she nearly fell over backward in shock.

She later shared with me that not only was she surprised that I knew her name, but she was also in disbelief that I knew it was her birthday.

This CNA went on to tell me that in her 15-year career she had never worked at a place where the CEO knew her name or personally acknowledged her!

Later in my career, I was sitting in the office of one of my executives when I noticed a card nestled on a wall shelf in between a picture of his kids and a picture of his spouse. As I took a closer look, I realized it was the birthday card I had given him over six months ago!

After these occurrences and many others like it, I've learned the power and impact a simple birthday message can have. The few minutes it takes to handwrite a birthday card and deliver it has always been worth the effort.

Though there are many ways to create a simple system to stay on top of this, I'll quickly share mine in hopes that you will see how easy it can be.

First, my HR director would e-mail me a list of birthdays for the upcoming month a few days before the new month started. Next, I created an ongoing reminder in my calendar for the end of each day to check the birthday list and write any cards I needed to write for the following day. Once I had written them, I would make sure to leave them on the middle of my desk when I left for the day so I'd immediately see them in the morning. Finally, I would take a few moments to deliver the birthday cards to my team members once I arrived at work.

Over the years I've learned I am not alone in having the kinds of experiences I've described above when handing out personal birthday cards and recognizing my team members on their special day. A simple sincere expression of gratitude and recognition on someone's birthday can quickly elevate the engagement level of your team and increase the strength of your culture.

#7

Hold One-on-One Meetings

If you've been a leader for a while, you may be familiar with the widely known personal assessment called *StrengthsFinder*. This assessment was first introduced in the popular book *Now, Discover Your Strengths*. In this book, authors Marcus Buckingham and Donald O. Clifton state, "The best mechanism for channeling the employee's path toward performance [is] regular, predictable, and productive meetings with his immediate supervisor." They later state that "these meetings with a manager are extraordinarily powerful" and "are a core regiment of strong organizations."

I agree. Having regular one-on-one interactions with your direct reports can totally change their experience at work and increase their level of performance. There is almost no more powerful way to build culture and alignment among your team than spending meaningful time with them in one-on-one settings.

For leaders, these meetings should have two primary objectives. The first is to establish clarity. You want to eliminate any ambiguity around the purpose, values, goals, expectations, performance, and standards of the organization.

The second is to build rapport and foster a relationship with those you lead.

When the meeting ends, the employee should feel valued, connected, and clear on what matters most.

A leader can achieve the objectives of the meeting by getting to know something new about the person, listening, sharing genuine care and concern for their success, providing guidance and coaching, clarifying expectations, reminding them of the mission and values, and providing honest feedback on performance.

Too often, good people leave an organization because of their relationship with their boss. Having regular one-on-one meetings will help you develop a strong relationship that can lead your team to much greater results. No matter how busy a leader is, these meetings are always time well spent.

Story

Several years back, one of my department heads was struggling with her performance. She just couldn't seem to measure up to the expectations we had for her department. However, through regular and consistent one-on-one meetings, we were able to put some simple systems and plans in place, together, to help her succeed.

In time, this department head became a big contributor to our success. She also became a champion of our culture.

One-on-one meetings provide leaders with a vehicle to constantly reinforce clarity and provide consistent feedback.

How long these meetings last and how often they occur depends on your specific circumstances and needs; however, even a monthly 15-minute meeting with both parties fully engaged can have a tremendous impact on your culture.

Most everyone recognizes leaders are busy. When leaders are willing to set aside time in their busy schedules to sit down with their team members on a regular basis, it sends a clear message that they are valued and important.

Don't miss out on the opportunity to build a stronger organizational culture by holding regular one-on-one meetings with your direct reports.

#8

Do Daily Rounds

Walking around your place of work is a simple yet extremely effective way to build culture in your organization and among your team. It is also a great opportunity to demonstrate idea #3 (be an example) and implement idea #4 (learn names).

To make your rounds less intimidating to your team, and to ensure people don't feel micromanaged, your primary purpose for these rounds should always be to strengthen your relationships with your team members and to help them feel cared about and known.

Story

When I worked at a health care center that provided around-the-clock care, the very first thing I did each morning was make a round on the floor and say good morning to my team. And at the end of each day, no matter how late it was, I made sure to do a quick round to say hello to my second shift (afternoon) staff. In time, I was amazed how this simple consistent act strengthened the relationships and bonds I had with my people. People knew me, and they knew I cared. I knew them and genuinely looked forward to saying hello to them each day.

One outstanding staff member I saw most mornings during my daily round shared with me that she was being heavily recruited by a competitor. After several attempts to lure her away with a much higher pay rate than we could offer her at the time, she confessed she wouldn't leave because I was the only CEO she had worked with that checked on her each morning to see how her day was going.

The easiest way to get to know your team while doing rounds is to ask them simple questions such as: "How'd your morning go?", "How was your weekend?", "Did you do anything interesting after work yesterday?", or "What has been the most exciting part of your day thus far?" These simple, nonthreatening questions open a door to conversations that help you to get to know more about those you lead. When you show genuine interest in the lives of those you lead, they will want to do their best and be successful.

Besides strengthening relationships with your team, there are other obvious benefits that come from doing daily rounds.

For one, daily rounds give you a chance to get a pulse on your team and gauge how they are doing. Do people seem happy, productive, and engaged, or is there tension, stress, and apathy written on their faces?

Another benefit is that rounds allow you to observe what is going on firsthand. Are people getting along and working together? Does it seem your team is providing great customer service and interacting with clients appropriately?

Finally, rounds allow you to have more of a presence with your team, giving you ample opportunities to offer assistance, training, guidance, motivation, and encouragement.

If you work with a team that is remote or doesn't meet at the same location, there are other ways to reach out and touch base. A simple daily text message, phone call, or e-mail can let your people know you care and are interested in them. This can help you develop a similarly strong relationship as you would by walking around your place of work.

As mentioned previously, people want to be known at work, especially by their leaders. Daily rounds provide great opportunities to get to know your team without any sort of formalities, awkwardness, or obligations. They also give you plenty of clues as to how people are feeling about work and performing.

Greeting your team every day—day in and day out—communicates a powerful message of care, concern, and unity. This simple habit strengthens culture in ways that will surprise you.

#9

Write Thank-You Notes

People want to feel recognized and appreciated. Period. Though it takes only a few minutes to do and costs virtually nothing, writing thank-you notes can have a big impact on your organization's culture and your reputation as a leader. This is such a simple act, but often leaders are too busy to consistently make it happen. Or they have someone do it for them. Committing yourself to writing at least three sincere thank-you notes a week can help you begin building the culture you want and need in your organization.

Story

I learned about an executive who would start each week by writing thank-you notes to his team. He developed the habit of arriving earlier to the office than normal each Monday morning, and he would spend that time writing several thank-you notes. Focusing on appreciating his staff from the very beginning of the week changed how this leader felt about his team and how he showed up each week. As you might imagine, his team loved working for him.

As leaders, we are often wired to point out the bad; however, taking time to write thank-you notes consistently forces you to really look for the good and validate and appreciate what others are doing.

A thank-you note not only changes the person who receives it, but also changes you.

Performance increases and stress levels go down when a thank-you note is written and received. Give it a try and pay attention to how a sincere thank-you note engages and energizes your team members.

#10

Create a Loyalty Program

Imagine an organization that always recognizes their employees when they complete another year of employment at the company. For example, to celebrate each employee's annual work anniversary, the leader of the company calls them up in front of their applauding peers, shakes their hand, talks about their tremendous example of loyalty and dedication to the team, and then hands them a small token of appreciation.

Now imagine a very different organization. One where tenure is never mentioned, and no one seems to notice or care when someone has completed another year of service at the company. An organization where everyone is basically clueless about how long others have been a part of the team. And if anyone ever asks, the leaders seem to shrug their shoulders as if the question is irrelevant and unimportant.

Which of these two organizations would you rather be a part of? And which one do you believe you'd be inclined to stay at longer?

Too many organizations don't recognize staff for remaining loyal to the company. This is a mistake!

With so many organizations struggling to hold on to their valuable team members, a simple loyalty program can offer relief. And making sure your team is recognized and appreciated for sticking with the team can really improve your culture.

A company loyalty program is all about recognizing employees on their annual employment anniversary (the date they first started at the organization). And for this program to be effective, it doesn't require elaborate or expensive gifts. In fact, a simple certificate of recognition signed by the CEO combined with some acknowledgment and public recognition in front of their peers can go a long way.

To ensure your people know you value those who stay at your company, make this recognition program widely known throughout the organization. And if you do give special gifts or other rewards for milestone anniversaries (e.g. one-year, five-year, 10-year, 20-year anniversaries), make it known. Loyalty programs aren't effective if people don't know about them or if they are done quietly under the radar.

Story

One supervisor mentioned to a valuable team member that he was sad she was leaving when she was so close to earning her one-year anniversary recognition and gold member award. The employee was unsure what he meant, and only after she had decided to leave the company did she learn about its loyalty program and the perks that came along with it. She shared that had she known about the award and perks, she would have stayed longer and completed at least a year of employment with the company.

Another time, a successful colleague of mine was offered a good job elsewhere after working for our company for over four years. Though the new offer was attractive, she told me she turned it down because she knew at her five-year anniversary she'd be earning the five-year company clock award along with the recognition that came with it. To her, this was an important milestone and accomplishment. It was enough to convince her to stay.

There are some logistics you must iron out and get right to make this type of program successful. For example, you'll need to decide when you will recognize staff. Will it be first thing in the morning on the exact date of their employment anniversary, or perhaps in a monthly all-staff meeting?

You'll also need to determine who will be responsible for ensuring the token of appreciation and/or award is ready to go the day the team member will be recognized. The last thing you want to do is be inconsistent in implementing this program by recognizing some while forgetting about others.

Finally, you need to make sure someone is staying on top of anniversary days and notifying others involved with carrying out the program so that, again, no one is ever missed.

Having a clear and simple recognition system for team member loyalty will communicate that you value commitment to your team. It will also help your people feel valued and important to your organization.

In the end, this type of program will extend the length of employment for some of your team members, and, more importantly, it will add to the strength of your culture.

#11

Set Team Goals and Track Progress

If a leader hopes to create a unified team, they must set clear team goals. Sure, there may also be different departmental and individual goals established, however team goals must trump all others. Leaders and employees must also be collectively responsible to achieve these team goals.

Rather than creating team goals, many leaders mistakenly establish only individual goals for different department leaders that pertain only to their specific department's areas of responsibility. When this happens, these individual goals often compete with one another and create misalignment, confusion, and power struggles. This results in individual departments and team members becoming concerned only about their own success, rather than staying focused on achieving results for the whole organization.

Clear team goals that everyone is collectively responsible for achieving create alignment around the organization's vision for success. However, simply establishing these team goals is not enough.

Once team goals are set, leaders must then establish a simple way to display and track progress toward reaching them. Doing this keeps everyone motivated and moving in the right direction.

Consistently updating progress toward goals helps improve organizational communication and clarity around the things that matter most.

Story

When I served as a CEO at a skilled nursing center, our leadership team established 15 clear, easy-to-track team goals. These goals included areas such as our census (patient volume), expense control, employee turnover, the number of on-the-job injuries, and customer satisfaction. These were goals that would help us drive our overall performance and live our mission and values.

We posted a list of these goals in our leadership conference room and near the time clock in the main employee breakroom.

Each month, I'd post an update of our month's progress toward reaching our goals. I also took time to share monthly updates on our team goals at every monthly all-staff meeting.

After having this system in place for many months, one of my most memorable moments as a leader happened at one of our all-staff meetings. A team member who did not have direct responsibilities for one of our team goals offered to help those who did have more direct responsibilities for that specific goal.

This willingness to help wherever needed to accomplish our team goals spread and led to many productive discussions about finding the best ways to ensure we reached all of our goals. As you might imagine, to my delight, this team achieved incredible results.

Establishing team goals that everyone is collectively responsible for, making them highly visible, and frequently providing progress updates will help keep everyone aligned and clear on what good performance looks like in your organization.

Adopting this simple practice consistently will set clear standards for the organization and bolster your culture in a big way!

#12

Have All-Staff Meetings

All-staff meetings are often the one time a leader has each month (or week or quarter) to share a message their entire team will hear. The most meaningful all-staff meetings highlight the organization's mission and values, helping to remind the team of what matters most. All-staff meetings also provide a great venue for updating the team on progress toward collective goals and rallying them around the most important initiatives at the time. Depending on the size of your team, this also can be a perfect opportunity to celebrate birthdays and employment anniversaries.

All-staff meetings should be all about creating clarity, showing appreciation and recognition, and celebrating. Strongly encourage your entire staff to participate and make sure all have an opportunity to tune in.

Depending on the size or nature of your organization, these meetings may need to be broadcast through video conferencing or on a call. Recording them and making them available on demand for a short while after the meeting is also a good idea.

Holding all-staff meetings on a regular basis allows a leader to share an inspiring and unifying message that leaves little room for ambiguity or confusion. It's an effective and easy way to create clarity and alignment across the entire team.

Story

I once worked at a very large hospital where the CEO held monthly town hall meetings. Though it was fun to be live in the large conference room where the meeting was held, staff members could also participate in a variety of ways so they wouldn't miss out.

During these regular meetings the CEO shared the latest updates on the hospital's strategy and goals. He also reiterated the vision and values of the organization.

This regular meeting with the CEO was motivating and kept everyone informed and on the same page. Employees felt valued knowing their leader was taking time to frequently share a message with them and many looked forward to his message.

Besides allowing everyone to hear the same messages from their leaders, a regular all-staff meeting also brings people together and invites them to rub shoulders with their co-workers. Thus, a regular all-staff meeting not only helps build trust in the company's leaders, but it can also foster relationships. When done right, all-staff meetings can set the tone for your company's culture.

To ensure your all-staff meetings provide a good experience for your team, there a few things to keep in mind.

First, the meetings should provide predominantly positive messages. This isn't a time to rail against your team for the transgressions of a few. For example, don't get after everyone for not showing up to work on time when there are only a few offenders in the crowd.

Second, be direct and to the point. Make your message clear and don't go on and on so that people become bored or annoyed. Try to share messages that are short and engaging.

Third, only share information that is relevant to all staff members. For example, don't talk about a new policy that only pertains to a specific department or dive into an issue that really should be discussed among a select group of employees.

Finally, leaders should avoid group discussions or brainstorming sessions during these all-staff gatherings, as doing so among such a large group is ineffective. Remember, the primary purposes of these all-staff meetings are to inform, motivate, and unify.

What if you aren't the CEO of your company and only lead a small team? You can still regularly bring together those who work under your leadership for all-staff meetings.

Also, for a remote workforce, holding a weekly, monthly, or quarterly all-staff video conference or call with a unifying message that keeps everyone informed and motivated can be just as effective as an in-person meeting.

Whether you are a part of a large organization or a small one, bring people together on a regular basis and communicate a message that supports your culture, exemplifies your values, and creates an excellent experience for all. A meaningful, consistent all-staff meeting can be a powerful accelerator toward strengthening your culture.

#13

Make Performance and Results Clear

Too many employees, whether unintentionally or not, are left to work in the dark. What I mean by this is that team members aren't sure about their company's or team's performance because no one ever lets them know. Though they might have an idea, it isn't always clear.

When teams are expected to work hard, but they aren't sure if all their hard work is paying off, it can be demoralizing. Very few people like to work in this type of environment. Most want to know exactly how their team is performing and what the results are from their efforts. The key here is transparency.

As leaders, we have a lot of information and knowledge about results that others don't. Sometimes it is easy to forget that our people are not as informed as we are, and so we fail to share information with them.

Other times we may realize our team is not well-informed, but we may wonder if taking the time to share results really matters to them.

This lack of clarity around results ends in feelings of uncertainty within an organization.

When leaders make a conscious effort to always inform their team members of results, performance improves.

When there is transparency and employees know where their team stands, it helps them feel informed, empowered, and valued. It also builds a sense of ownership and belonging within the organization.

Story

Kristina, a department head who worked for me at a health care center, didn't like to lose. When I began sharing data about each department's monthly performance with my entire team, and Kristina's department wasn't at the top, she instantly wanted to improve.

Kristina and I had conversations about how to increase performance, and before long, her department was consistently performing at the top. This inspired other leaders to also elevate performance in their own departments.

A different health care executive I worked with didn't take time to show the financial metrics and performance data to his team of nurses. He figured they'd find most of the information boring, and he reasoned that nurses weren't interested in financial stuff.

Though I agreed financial performance may not be their top concern, I knew it would be interesting to them to see how the health care center was doing from a financial perspective.

After encouragement, this executive began to share more financial performance information with his team of nurses, and he was surprised by how they responded. Not only did most of them find the information interesting, but they also began to ask questions and offer great ideas on how they could cut costs, increase revenue, and improve the quality of care and the financial results.

These nurses engaged further at work when they knew more about the organization's performance and results.

Consistently sharing results with your team on a regular basis not only can inspire them, but also provides you with ample opportunities to help your staff know what they can do to accelerate performance. When well-informed, most staff members will work more diligently to improve results.

Most team members want to be in the know at work and most want to be a part of a winning team. Don't make the mistake of assuming your people are knowledgeable about the team's results. Take the time to always make results clear and you will be surprised how performance improves and your culture is strengthened.

#14

Actively Participate in New Employee Orientation

In a lot of ways, new employee orientation (NEO) gives leaders the opportunity to create raving fans and loyal followers from the very beginning of employment. Why does NEO present such an opportunity?

First, new employees are generally excited about a new job and sincerely want to perform well. Sometimes this excitement and desire can wane quickly; however, leaders can capitalize on and prolong these feelings by providing a great start through NEO.

Second, most new hires come to NEO prepared to listen. They want to know more about their new company and how they can fit in and contribute. They also want to be able to feel good about and perhaps even brag about who they are now working for. When NEO doesn't deliver on these desires, and when leaders don't ensure it's structured in a way that will create a positive experience, and when the most inspirational and important information about the company is not the focal point of the event, it can be a letdown.

Finally, first impressions matter. NEO sets the tone for each new team member's employment experience with your organization. The feelings new team members feel at NEO will often linger, and when done right can influence their entire experience with your company. In many ways, NEO can make or break the initial engagement level of your newest team members as they begin working.

The primary purposes of NEO should be to create clarity around those things that matter most to your organization and to immerse the new team members in your unique culture. Thus, the organization's mission and purpose, standards and core values, and objectives and goals should be emphasized, lived, explained, and reinforced throughout the event.

One big mistake leaders often make with NEO is that they delegate this important function to others in the organization and then stay entirely out of the process. Instead, leaders should take an active role in both the development and implementation of the NEO procedures. They must ensure that this one-time event for every new employee clarifies and reinforces the culture they want to build and cultivate within the organization.

At the very minimum, I recommend leaders present on the meaning and importance of the company's mission, vision, and values during the NEO proceedings. These items are too critical to delegate to others.

Story

As a new manager, I attended a new employee orientation at a large medical center where the CEO spent a significant amount of time with the new team members. He shared the hospital's history, vision, mission, core values, and the most important goals. He hung around most of the day even when he wasn't presenting, and he invited everyone to breakfast with him in the executive suite the following day. He showed a genuine desire to get to know new staff.

As a new manager at this hospital, I felt connected right away. NEO at this medical center also made me incredibly excited about where I was working and who I was working for.

When I later became the CEO of a healthcare center, I found that following the example of this leader paid off. I spent a lot of time in my NEOs, and I shared the organization's history, mission, vision, core values, and goals. I also enjoyed lunch with each new group who started.

I realized that my level of involvement at NEO as the CEO allowed me to shape my center's culture with every new employee.

Too many leaders and organizations don't capitalize on the eager and captive audience they have during NEO.

As a leader, don't shy away from meaningful opportunities to connect with your people and establish the culture you want. Take full advantage of NEO by playing an active role in it—both in its design and implementation—and you will heavily influence the culture within your organization.

#15

Offer a Raise on the First Day of Employment

This suggestion is all about bribery and an attempt to "buy" engagement and credibility on someone's first day. (I'm joking—I only wish it were that easy!) Actually, it's something very different than that.

After explaining the organization's mission, vision, and core values in new employee orientation, leaders and organizations can emphasize their importance to the company by offering a certain percent raise to any team member who memorizes the organization's values (along with their definitions) and the mission and vision statements.

Story

At a health care center I led, several people earned a raise by memorizing our core values, mission, and vision. Let me share one example.

Ashley was a young mother of two who worked hard as a certified nursing assistant to provide for her children. I noticed she had a quiet determination

63

about her during new employee orientation, and when I explained that every employee had an opportunity for an immediate raise, I could tell I had piqued her interest.

Out of all our new employees, Ashley had every excuse not to complete this task. Besides being a single mom who worked more than one job, she had always struggled in school.

Through sheer willpower and grit, Ashley was able to memorize our mission, vision, and values and earn her raise. I was so excited for her! I wanted to know more about how she did it; so, I asked.

Ashley shared that she had recorded herself reading our mission, vision, and values and listened to it while she slept, drove to work, showered, and whenever and wherever she could. This went on for about five months until one day, she said, it was stuck in her head. I was impressed!

Though it took her longer than she wanted, Ashley felt she had accomplished something great—and she had! I was extremely proud of her, and I knew memorizing our mission, vision, and values would help her perform better and add more value to our team.

Perhaps best of all, Ashley described how our mission and values were changing her perspective not just about how she approached work but also her life outside of work. This was a proud moment for me as leader.

Offering a raise from the start of employment is a wise investment that pays for itself. As new employees immerse in and engage with your culture more quickly than they otherwise would, as they begin producing results that are aligned with your culture at a higher level and sooner than expected, and as you grow the number of *culture champions* in your organization, the return on this invest will become clear.

This raise should also be a standing offer. Inevitably, down the road, individuals on your team will ask for a raise outside of your normal policies for pay increases. I loved reminding my team that they always had an opportunity to earn one by memorizing these important items when they hadn't done so already.

At the end of the day, this is a simple and effective way to reinforce those things that matter most in your organization. When you have a team that knows the mission, vision, and values of your organization, your culture will grow stronger. And even if most of your employees never take you up on the offer, extending it conveys how committed you are to them. This powerful message alone will boost your culture.

#16

Invite People to Quit

After you explain the unique and exciting culture that exists at your organization, invite people to quit. This may sound even stranger than the last idea, but hear me out.

To begin, you should know that Zappos, a company known for having a great work environment and culture, became somewhat famous for this practice. It was one way they were able to shape and cultivate the culture they wanted.

Story

For every Ashley (from the story in suggestion #15), there seems to always be someone who is just the opposite. Lina was another certified nursing assistant who attended our new employee orientation. With her arms folded and a frown on her face for much of the day, I could tell she wasn't thrilled to be there or impressed with what was shared.

At the close of orientation, I explained how—to accomplish our goals—it was important for everyone to be excited

> about what we were doing at our health care center and what we stood for. Next, I let the group know that if anyone was not enthusiastic about joining our team, I'd love to give them a $200 check to help them find a better fit.
>
> After her first day working on the floor, Lina came to my office to collect her check.

One reason why the concept of inviting people to quit is effective in bolstering your culture is because it reinforces that you are serious about the culture and will hold people to what matters most in your organization. It communicates clearly that building and protecting the company's culture is important to your organization.

Another reason why it is effective is because almost nothing can bring your company's culture down faster than someone who doesn't buy into the culture or want to be a part of it. The quicker you can identify these people and help them find a better fit elsewhere, the quicker your organizational culture will improve.

No matter the dollar amount your organization decides to offer people who realize they are not in the right place, I've learned that in the long run, it will always cost less than what it would cost to keep them around.

Now, to be sure that I am clear: this practice shouldn't be about getting rid of people who may challenge current practices, ask questions, or otherwise create disharmony or conflict. Rather, it's about ensuring everyone is surrounded by others who are passionate about the vision, values, and purpose of the organization, and what the team as a whole is trying to accomplish.

Too many organizations and leaders do a disservice to people who are mismatched and unhappy at work by keeping them around longer than they should. Helping people find a new place to work that will be a better fit for them shows compassion and will strengthen your company's culture.

#17

Improve Your Meetings

As one of the most basic functions of any organization, meetings often aren't given the attention they deserve in shaping an organization's culture. The quality of your meetings can play a pivotal role.

Regrettably, most people disdain meetings, and it's hard to blame them. Meetings are often poorly run and poorly structured—thus, participants leave feeling like they've wasted their time.

There are two ways every leader can and should improve their meetings:

One, the purpose of every meeting must always be clear. When there is a clear understanding of why the meeting exists and why it is essential and important, people can understand why it must take place. When the core objective of the meeting is clear, nonessential and inappropriate discussions are replaced with relevant ones. When team members clearly understand what they are trying to accomplish in a meeting, their interest level in the meeting increases.

Making the purpose of a meeting clear doesn't happen by simply stating it once. In fact, it's a good idea to remind everyone of the purpose of the meeting at the beginning of each and every one. This will create clarity around the meeting and instantly invite participants to engage.

Two, roles must be well-defined in meetings. If people don't know their part in the meeting, they will probably wonder why they are there. Or, even worse, they may play the wrong role and slow down or disrupt the meeting's flow. When people know their part—how they should participate and contribute in the meeting—they will become much more involved.

Knowing roles also helps meetings run much more efficiently. Let's face it: people get frustrated when meetings are inefficient and full of redundancy. Clearly defining roles helps eliminate the duplication of efforts that often exists during meetings.

If a meeting does not have a clear purpose, it should be discontinued, and if a staff member does not have a clear role in a meeting, they shouldn't attend. Otherwise, the hunch that meetings are a complete waste of time becomes legitimate.

Story

When I arrived as the CEO of a health care center, I quickly learned that the current leadership team dreaded meetings. And there was one meeting that was the most despised of all; however, it was extremely important to the results at the center.

After some open discussion with the leaders who participated in this dreaded meeting, I realized most didn't understand why the meeting had to take place or why it mattered so much to our success as a health care center. I also discovered most didn't understand their role in the meeting.

As I helped people understand the purpose of the meeting and we clearly defined their roles, the meeting became much more effective and enjoyable. And although not everyone learned to absolutely love this meeting, some did, and everyone learned to appreciate its importance.

Once the purpose of the meeting and each person's roles were made clear, rarely did anyone complain again about the meeting.

As an essential activity in all organizations, there is no denying that good meetings—where the purpose is always clear and roles are well-defined—will strengthen its culture.

#18

Provide Measurement

Everyone likes to know how they are performing at work and how they are being evaluated. Without clarity around these important items, people will be left to constantly wonder whether they are doing a good job.

This lack of clarity may lead to some of your best performers believing they are failing, while some of your worst performers might think they are excelling. For this reason, leaders should find simple ways to provide measurement.

Story

Tara was a receptionist responsible for responding to customers at a health care center I was helping. During one of the leadership meetings, the team decided the center's response time to customers needed improvement to help increase performance at the center. So, the CEO of the center bought Tara a stopwatch, set some goals with her, and asked her to begin timing and tracking how quickly she returned calls to customers.

Though a little hesitant at first, Tara soon embraced this new way of doing things and quickly exceeded expectations. Not only did response times greatly improve with Tara now tracking them, but she also became more engaged and seemed happier at work.

By setting some goals and tracking her response time, Tara now instantly knew each day whether she was doing a good job.

Another health care leader I worked with set up clear measurements for his team of certified nursing assistants (CNAs), which included attendance and punctuality performance, response times to call lights, and customer satisfaction results. Each metric had goals associated with it, and each morning this leader posted a ranking of his CNAs for each category as well as an overall ranking based on a combination of the three.

This allowed each CNA the opportunity to see where they ranked among their peers and how they were performing based on the established goals.

This system dramatically improved results as well as the engagement level of his team of CNAs.

Most employees worry that their performance will be evaluated by subjective metrics and the opinions of others. Providing clear objective measurements gives employees the peace of mind that they will be assessed based on their performance.

The value of knowing how you are being evaluated and how you are performing at work is priceless when it comes to employee satisfaction.

Now, you may have to be a little creative from time to time on how to provide measurement for everyone you lead. But this shouldn't keep you from finding ways for every team member to measure and gauge their performance.

Providing clear measurements for each of your team members will improve your team's level of motivation and enthusiasm at work and strengthen your culture.

#19

Utilize Your Suggestion Box

At face value, a suggestion box offers your team a safe and easy way to share feedback and ideas. It provides an opportunity for employees to have a voice and add their input into the organization.

When looking more deeply, providing a suggestion box speaks volumes to how you feel about those you lead. It communicates that you are interested in their thoughts and find value in asking for their insights.

A suggestion box can also show you are open to new ideas and willing to listen to your team. However, all of this is only true if two important things happen:

One, you must regularly share some suggestions that come through the box, along with what you have done or will do in response. This doesn't mean you must share every suggestion—in fact, doing so is a bad idea. Instead, share just enough to remind people about the suggestion box and to show you are taking feedback seriously. A good time to do this may be during all-staff meetings.

Two, you must not only remind people that it's there and always available to them, but you must also be clear about how often you will check it. This can be communicated verbally, but you should also post a highly visible sign near the box that clearly indicates exactly when and how often the box will be checked. This is important.

Story

At one point, the suggestion box at a health care center where I worked became somewhat of a complaint box, and that was OK. People were able to express their frustrations and be heard. It also gave us plenty of chances to evaluate things and make improvements.

One day, several employees complained about the practices of one particular nurse through the suggestion box. We were able to investigate the complaints and take care of a situation before it became too serious.

This simple suggestion box not only saved our organization from a lot of potential risk that day, but it also served as a constant reminder that our team had a voice and would be heard.

The suggestion box should be in a highly visible, easily accessible area, such as next to a breakroom entrance or by a time clock. In my experience, many of the suggestions received can be invaluable.

If your team is remote or works in different locations, an electronic suggestion box with an anonymous e-mail address or even a hotline number can be set up to solicit feedback. These methods of receiving feedback from your team can be just as effective, especially when advertised and utilized properly.

Now, many leaders state they've tried a suggestion box in the past and have seen little to no value come of it. This is often because they've failed to do the two important items mentioned earlier.

A suggestion box is a form of upward communication that can improve a work environment. However, if you aren't committed to reviewing suggestions, sharing a few on a consistent basis, or acting on those ideas that can help your business, don't do it. It can be demoralizing for employees if they believe all suggestions are ignored.

Many people don't like speaking up, but if given a different avenue to communicate, they will. When done right with consistency, good communication, and follow-through, a suggestion box can and will strengthen your culture.

#20

Say "I Don't Know" and "I'm Sorry"

Vulnerability from a leader builds trust. Trust is essential for teamwork. And teamwork is essential for having a strong culture that produces results. The two best phrases that demonstrate vulnerability from a leader are "I don't know" and "I'm sorry."

Many leaders pretend they have all the answers, and it's hard to blame them, really. In many ways, our society teaches us that a leader should have all the answers.

Additionally, many leaders act as if they don't make mistakes. Much like the false narrative about having all the right answers, leaders tend to believe they shouldn't show their weaknesses or admit any miscues.

The truth is no leader has all the right answers, and all leaders make mistakes. Everyone knows this!

Also, people can usually detect when you don't know something, and they can normally recognize when you make a mistake. When a leader fails to say "I don't know" or "I'm sorry," they aren't fooling anyone (expect maybe themselves). Therefore, why not be honest and own it?

Refusing to admit you don't know something or that you made a mistake only results in frustration and diminished respect for you as a leader. Worst of all, it inadvertently

79

sends a message that avoiding vulnerability by acting like you know it all or never make mistakes is the way to behave in the organization. And, to reiterate, a lack of vulnerability squashes trust and teamwork.

Being vulnerable by saying "I don't know" and "I'm sorry" will endear you to your team and build confidence in your leadership. Though some leaders may doubt it, saying these two phrases when appropriate gives you credibility.

Story

When I first started as a manager in the health care industry, I was pretty clueless about a lot of things. Though I had some experience and schooling and felt good about my leadership and business acumen, there were so many health care acronyms and unfamiliar clinical terms. I felt lost at times and a little worried my team might reject such an inexperienced leader in the industry.

Thankfully, I had a great team surrounding me, and I had the courage to ask them a lot of questions. Although I was the person *in charge*, this team helped me learn the industry.

Because I was vulnerable and openly admitted I didn't know it all and often had to say "I'm sorry" for my many mistakes, my team felt comfortable being vulnerable and asking me questions as well and admitting their missteps.

As you might expect, our team became very tight knit as we depended and relied on each other. Because we were mutually vulnerable, this built a strong sense of unity and trust, which trickled down to others in the organization and really solidified our culture.

My willingness as a leader to say "I don't know" and "I'm sorry" created the closest team I have ever been a part of at work. And our results? They far surpassed anyone's expectations, including my own.

When a leader is willing to be vulnerable first, others will follow. Without vulnerability from a leader it is nearly impossible to build the cohesive team that is needed to produce a strong culture and achieve stellar results.

#21

Frequently Solicit Feedback on Your Performance

To continue on the vulnerability train (introduced in suggestion #20), here is another suggestion that will help. Though it can be uncomfortable, one of the most powerful ways to be vulnerable and impact those you lead is to frequently ask them how you can improve as their leader. This can be done through formal reviews and surveys or simply by verbally asking during leadership meetings and other interactions with your team. In the beginning you may not get much response, but continuing to ask will show you mean it.

When you do finally get that precious bit of feedback, make sure you consider how to use it to improve. It is also helpful to share the feedback with your leadership team and point out what you have changed or are trying to change as a result of the feedback. This will demonstrate even more your willingness to be vulnerable and build trust. It will also open the door to more feedback that can help you be the best leader you can possibly be.

Story

Cindy was my director of marketing and very good at her job. During a one-on-one meeting with her I asked what I could do to be a better leader, and she told me. She candidly said I needed to provide clearer, more effective direction to her and other department heads so the team could function better.

Though it stung for a moment, I knew Cindy was right, and I worked to improve. This feedback helped me be a better leader and increased the level of trust we shared. It also allowed me to show Cindy and the team that I valued their opinions and viewed my colleagues as important members of the organization.

Since this conversation with Cindy, I've shared this story many times to convey I'm serious about feedback.

Once you begin asking for and receiving feedback and then show you are striving to improve, others will follow your example. Within time, giving and receiving feedback on performance will become part of your culture. This will also send a message that everyone is expected to do all they can to help the organization improve and succeed, even if it means calling out the CEO!

Without a willingness to be vulnerable and encourage feedback, it is difficult to build a team that is unified and working toward creating a strong organizational culture.

#22

Tell People Their Job Is Significant

One of the worst beliefs to have is that what you do at work really doesn't matter. Most people want to know they are helping make a difference in another human being's life, even if it is only a co-worker or boss. When your people view their job as insignificant, it can lead to a considerable amount of dread and unfulfillment at work.

Verbalizing often (every day when possible) that each team member's job is important and significant can completely change the atmosphere within your company.

Story

Ron was an afternoon housekeeper at a skilled nursing center I helped. His primary duties were to take out heavy bags of trash and sweep and mop what must have felt like endless corridor floors. Day after day, however, I noticed he came to work with a big, friendly smile and a positive attitude.

Soon, I recognized I could tell when Ron was in the building because the entire mood on the floor instantly improved. I admired Ron for the way he went about his job and carried himself.

One day, I complimented Ron on his work, and this started a memorable conversation. I asked him why he came to work so enthusiastic each day, and he proudly informed me it was because he knew he was making a difference.

Wanting to learn more, I asked him how he knew he was making a difference and why he thought maybe others who were doing similar tasks didn't feel the same way he did. He told me it was because he had worked for a supervisor who reminded him daily that his work mattered.

Though I only helped at the center for a few weeks, Ron had taught me a valuable lesson.

All of us have an intrinsic need to make a difference. When your people do not feel their work is contributing or adding value for others, they will develop low morale. Thus, leaders must help their team understand how their specific role makes a difference and how it ties to the company's mission and purpose.

Helping your people never lose sight of their impact in your organization matters. When people believe their job is significant, and you remind them often, your organization's culture will grow stronger.

#23

Hold a Short Daily Morning Meeting

One of the best ways to align team members and help everyone focus on what matters most is by having a quick daily morning meeting with the leaders in your organization. The meeting should be short, concise, and focused on priorities and goals for the day.

Many teams that implement such a meeting call them "stand-up meetings" because they literally do not allow people to sit down and get comfortable. The idea is they should not last longer than 10 to 15 minutes at most.

The primary purposes of this meeting are information sharing and alignment. Minor issues that can distract a team from their most important priorities can easily be resolved by meeting together quickly each day. Likewise, when your team members know they can handle small issues at the daily meeting, they will send out fewer e-mails and texts about small or trivial matters.

Story

A team I worked with was really struggling to communicate and be on the same page. Some worried about bothering or interrupting their co-workers; others felt they were too busy to get feedback and input, and some were only worried about what they believed was most important. As a result, this fragmented team ended up often making decisions in isolation, even when these decisions impacted others. This led to frustration, inefficiencies, and poor performance.

One day, the primary leaders of this team agreed it was critical to improve communication, so they decided to hold a quick daily morning meeting. Though they knew it would receive some initial backlash, they believed sticking with it would help.

During this meeting they focused on top priorities for the day as well as any updates or follow-up items from the previous day. They were also able to resolve small issues that needed quick answers. Soon enough, the team's performance greatly improved.

Rather than working in isolation, the quick daily meeting helps get everyone on the same page each morning. Hearing what others are working on for the day also allows a team to shift priorities and be more strategic about their daily work. Finally, relationships are developed and strengthened when a team meets each day. I've found that once implemented, in most instances, leaders soon look forward to the daily interactions as a group.

Since the meeting is designed to be short, avoid lengthy discussions or brainstorming about complex problems. This should be reserved for other meetings.

Additionally, to be most effective, this meeting should take place consistently, every day, regardless of who may or may not be in the office. For example, if the CEO has an appointment in the morning that he must attend, it shouldn't keep the rest of the team from meeting.

Holding a daily morning meeting consistently improves communication, increases efficiency, and cuts down on confusion. It aligns teams and helps them build better relationships with one another.

Though every business environment is different, finding a way to hold a quick daily morning meeting, even if it means having a video conference or call for remote teams, will really help strengthen your culture.

#24

Hire Smart

One of the most important decisions your organization makes is who to invite to join your team. Though the suggestion to "hire smart" is obvious, it surprises me how often companies and leaders continue to make poor hiring decisions and fail to change their process.

To hire smart, a leader must ensure first and foremost that their organization is hiring for fit. This must be the number one priority!

Instead of becoming enamored with a candidate because of their skills or experience, leaders must look past the resume. Someone who shares your values and will bring the attitude and characteristics your organization espouses is much better than someone who has a lot of great experience. Don't get me wrong; experience matters, but if the person is a misfit for your culture, their experience and skills will matter very little in the long run.

Likewise, too many organizations I've worked with become desperate and fill open positions quickly. As a result, they constantly end up regretting hiring decisions and find themselves trapped in what feels like an endless cycle of employee turnover.

To help you hire smart, avoid extending an offer of employment on the day of the interview. Slow down and allow yourself and your team some time to think about the commitment you are making to this new hire. Consider whether this person is someone everyone on the team can get behind and help support 100 percent once they begin.

Also, envision how this individual will contribute to the organization six months down the road. Will they still be around? How will they be influencing and impacting your culture? Do they have the potential to add significant value to your team?

Additionally, during the interview process, get out from behind the desk and take the candidate on a tour of your place of work. Introduce them to lots of their prospective co-workers, show them a typical workspace, and observe how they behave in the normal day-to-day work setting. This can help you evaluate whether the person will truly thrive in your culture.

Finally, make sure culture, including your company's mission and values, is a focal point of discussion during the interview process. Too often, leaders and companies don't explain what their culture is all about until after an employment offer is extended. This is too late! Help those you interview know you are serious about your culture and that candidates who aren't a good fit won't have a good employment experience.

Story

A skilled nursing center I'm familiar with transformed their culture by altering their interview process. Rather than investing extreme amounts of money and time into training, educating, coaching, disciplining, redirecting, and guiding new hires, they made the decision to put all their money, time, and effort into the front end of the process.

Their interview system was rigorous and included multiple interviews with different leaders and even several peers. The top-level leaders also made interviewing candidates a key priority and carved out time to meet and interview as many candidates as possible, regardless of the position they were applying for.

Candidates also had to shadow peers and participate in the work they would be doing if hired. This center made sure to hire smart and eventually had unbelievable success.

Remember: just because someone has the experience doesn't mean they will perform well for you. The first priority should be finding the right fit.

It probably goes without saying, but who you hire will have a tremendous impact on the strength of your culture.

#25

Create a Core Team

There are two common problems with most leadership teams.

First, they are too big to be effective. It's as if organizations have somehow gotten the idea that a good way to recognize individuals and make them feel important is to add them to the leadership team. While the desire to help others feel valued is noble, making a leadership team too big sacrifices its ability to work well. In the long run, adding nonessential people to the leadership team hurts everyone, as trying to make important decisions among a large group of people is nearly impossible.

Second, too many leadership teams are misaligned. Rather than working together to improve the results of the entire organization, they work in isolation and concentrate only on their own responsibilities and areas of expertise. For a leadership team to perform well, its members must share a broader view of the entire success of the company.

Furthermore, it isn't uncommon for leaders to have incentives, compensation packages, and even goals that compete with one another. This amplifies the discord and leads to infighting and fractured teams.

To overcome these two major problems, and to strengthen the organization's culture, a leader should form a smaller core team or executive team.

A core leadership team consists of anywhere between three to seven members at most. Including more people than that hinders the ability of everyone to weigh in and thus negatively affects decision-making and cohesion.

The members of the core team typically oversee the most important areas of responsibility within the company. These individuals normally have the biggest opportunities to influence the results of the entire organization.

Once a core team is created, they should share collective goals that supersede all others. They should also meet frequently. I recommend a weekly core team meeting, however twice a month may be sufficient based on your organization's needs and circumstances.

To hold effective core team meetings, start by asking each leader to share what they feel is the biggest area of opportunity to achieve the organization's goals, mission, and values. While each member of the team shares their answer, create a list. Once a list is written down with each person's insight, make a real-time agenda and begin by discussing the most critical items on the list first.

It won't be unusual to only cover one or two items during the meeting. When this happens, the others on the list will either need to wait for the next meeting, or, if urgent, another core team meeting can be held sooner than is typical to address the other important and pressing items.

The core team wrestles with the biggest decisions that must be made within the organization. They act as a sounding board or internal advisory board for the primary leader or CEO.

In order to make decisions that will stick, a leader should always invite the core team members into the decision-making process. Each should have a chance to voice their opinion, and healthy debate should abound. When done right, no major decision will be made without first consulting the core team.

This is vital to success because when key members on a leadership team buy in to and are unified around decisions made in the organization, others will notice and follow their lead. Thus, using a core team is essential to creating alignment and cohesion across the entire organization. Unity at the top of a company creates unity throughout.

Story

As a CEO of a health care center, my leadership team consisted of over 20 department heads, directors, and executives. This was too many people for effective discussions and decision-making, so I formed a "core team" of six leaders.

We met together often and made important decisions together. We didn't always agree, and we definitely participated in plenty of healthy debate. However, we stayed committed to being unified on all final decisions made by the group.

While working together, we made a very difficult decision to eliminate a service line our organization had been providing to the community for many years. We knew this decision would cause a lot of stress and heartache in the beginning, but in the end, we felt it would be the best choice for the long-term impact and success of our company.

Though not everyone on our core team initially supported the idea, after a lengthy discussion and looking at things together, we were all able to stand behind the decision to eliminate the service. We then worked together to develop and implement a plan.

The service shutdown process, which included referring many loyal clients to other health care institutions, was emotionally draining and difficult for everyone. Once completed, though, I realized the transition went about as smoothly and successfully as possible. I knew it was because the key leaders were united throughout the entire process, and this alignment had trickled down to the rest of the staff right when we needed it most. Together we succeeded in discontinuing this service line as quickly and effectively as we could.

If I had made this decision in isolation and asked others to simply fall in line or do what I asked, disaster surely would have ensued. However, using my core team, I was able to navigate through this and many other difficult changes that led our health care center to its best-ever performance.

When the leader of an organization brings together his or her key people and they act as a cohesive group, the unity flows throughout the organization and creates a strong culture that produces results.

#26

Celebrate

Few things have the potential to bring together a team more than celebrating. Whether it's a holiday, someone's birthday, or the achievement of a goal, making time to have fun and celebrate at work will improve your culture.

As we all know, people crave recognition. Celebration serves as another way to recognize your team.

Celebrations tied to performance are often the best kind. Of course, in most instances, the better the results, the bigger the celebration might be. (In suggestion #11, I talked about setting and tracking goals. If you combine that suggestion with this one by adding some type of team celebration when progress is made and goals are met, it will be a huge win for your culture.)

Celebrations don't have to be big or elaborate events. Some of the most memorable celebrations are the simplest. Even a small celebration can have a big impact on improving your culture.

Story

When I was the CEO at a health care center, we had outstanding results during a particular month. It was a busy time for us, and most of my team was stretched pretty thin, but I didn't want to fail to recognize our team for this achievement. So I purchased some small pins and handed them out to each staff member. These pins had the health care center's logo and read "Best Month Ever."

While handing out the pins, I wore one with pride, shared my appreciation with each team member, and told them how incredible the achievement was.

In the following months my team began to ask if they'd earned another pin. I was surprised by their reaction to my simple gesture of celebration.

Sure enough, after several months went by, our results surpassed the previous "best month ever." So, I found myself handing out new pins and more congratulatory high-fives. These pins became part of our culture and were one simple way we celebrated great results.

If performance is strong, finding reasons to celebrate is not too difficult. When performance is not so good, leaders should create smaller goals and still find ways to celebrate progress toward them.

Celebrations should occur more than once or twice a year. Some of the best organizations I've interacted with celebrate a lot. This makes work fun!

Besides recognition and fun, celebrations also provide team members an opportunity to relax and get to know each other. They can help foster tight-knit bonds and fortify relationships that aren't otherwise formed in normal day-to-day work.

You'll be surprised by how celebrating, even in simple ways, really matters to your people. When done right, celebrations make work enjoyable and can create memorable experiences that your people will share—and may never forget.

You can strengthen your culture by celebrating often!

#27

Do Frequent Satisfaction Surveys

If you care about your team members and want to make them a priority, you need to prove it. One way to do this is to request their feedback often through employee satisfaction surveys.

Employee satisfaction surveys provide invaluable insight into your team's perceptions about their work and areas the company can focus on to improve the employee experience. Though the rate at which you do them may vary, I highly recommend a quarterly satisfaction survey.

When done consistently, don't be surprised if a quarterly satisfaction survey causes your staff to roll their eyes and profess, "Again?!" This is actually a good thing. Not only does it give you another opportunity to explain why you are conducting the surveys so often, but it also means your people are noticing that you are serious about improving as an employer.

To fully leverage your efforts in conducting surveys, I recommend the following process:

First, make sure you share the results of the survey in a timely manner with the entire team. Everyone will know you've done a survey, so many will be curious to see what comes of it. Share the results with complete transparency. Include the good, the bad, and the ugly, because, after all, people know how they responded. (And most have an idea of how others responded as well.)

Second, once results are shared, act on them. Make plans to improve in one or two areas and then follow through with those plans.

Third, communicate widely with your entire team the changes you've made as a result of the feedback. When your team sees you have acted on what they've said, you will find that participation in future surveys will greatly increase. You will also notice a higher level of commitment among your team.

Finally, be sure to share why certain things may not change immediately despite the feedback received. Be open about it or suggest how together you might be able to make it happen.

Let me share a quick example. Let's say you receive a lot of comments about needing new computers in the office, but ordering new computers isn't currently financially feasible. Taking time to explain why it isn't possible now and what results would need to look like to make it happen in the future will build rapport, trust, and credibility.

Though some employee satisfaction surveys are certainly better than others, having one is better than having none. And there are so many ways to make these surveys happen. You can hire someone from outside your organization or create one on your own. The most important thing of all is that you do them.

Story

A health care center I worked at had unusually high turnover. This led to what felt like an endless list of open positions and a constant need to recruit and hire new staff.

Things started to change, however, when the center began to conduct quarterly satisfaction surveys and act on them. Once a survey was completed, the leaders did a great job communicating the results as well as how they were going to make changes to improve.

Within two years of consistently following this practice, this center was recognized as a top place to work in the industry and had a stack of applicants who wanted to work there.

By being consistent and diligent about the simple process of conducting surveys frequently, sharing results, acting on those results, and then communicating changes made, great things happen. Conducting regular employee satisfaction surveys—while providing a clear explanation of why you do them so often—will strengthen your culture.

#28

Love

When we are honest with ourselves, nothing brings people together and makes them want to do their best more than love. Love for others is a powerful leadership quality.

If you don't love the people you work with or love what you do, you need to find a way to get there. Love from a leader *transforms* organizations. Love your work, love your company, and most importantly, love those you lead.

How do you show love? You can start by implementing many of the suggestions found in this book. Conversely, their effectiveness will be impacted by the love your people perceive as you implement them. If you show up in a way that demonstrates you sincerely care about your people, the simple suggestions offered in this book will have the ability to change the entire direction of your organization.

Story

On Thursday, August 24th, 2017, weather experts predicted that a major hurricane with unprecedented rainfall would hit southeast Texas. I had the responsibility of overseeing 10 skilled nursing centers in the area. As you can imagine, I was worried about what might happen. We did our best to prepare for the worst.

One of my centers near the coast needed to evacuate prior to the storm; they moved all their patients to a building that was more inland. The other centers hunkered down to wait out the storm.

Many of my executives and leaders lived in these skilled nursing centers for days— and some even weeks—before returning to their own homes to assess damages. In this time of crisis, these dedicated leaders worked side-by-side with their staff, preparing beds, cooking meals, and doing laundry. They also encouraged their teams to get rest, eat, take breaks, and go home if possible while they themselves worked diligently around the clock to keep patients safe, comfortable, and out of harm's way.

The love demonstrated by many of these heroic health care leaders at this desperate time was extraordinary. Did the staff members who received so much support from their leaders know they loved them? Yes! And you can guess how these teams responded to these leaders after their selfless acts of dedication, sacrifice, and service during this devastating natural disaster.

When you choose to love those you lead and show up in a way that demonstrates genuine care and concern—day in and day out—your culture will be strong, and reaching the goals you hope to achieve as an organization will become inevitable.

Conclusion

The strength of a culture in any organization is shaped first and foremost by the person in charge, and most often by the small and simple things they do. A leader's responsibility in strengthening a culture cannot be downplayed, nor can it be delegated to others. A leader must do the little things that matter most.

If you are serious about creating a strong culture, develop the discipline and fortitude to do the simple things offered in this book. Take one or two of the suggestions and begin to implement them right away, then build on those by adding more.

Remember the little trim tab and its capacity to redirect a large ship. Do not discredit the impact small actions will have on the lives of those you lead.

The simple ideas in this book have been provided as a way to remind you of how you can best strengthen your culture and improve your results as a leader.

I'm convinced that nothing is more important to your own personal fulfillment at work, as well as your success as a leader, than the strength of your organization's culture.

Many of the suggestions offered in this book have been presented only at surface level. To learn more about the information and suggestions provided, or if I can help you implement any of these ideas within your team or organization, please connect with me on LinkedIn, visit TheCenterforCompanyCulture.com, or e-mail me at Tim@TheCenterforCompanyCulture.com.

The Center for
Company Culture

TheCenterforCompanyCulture.com

Tim Burningham is an experienced manager, leader, and CEO. He has led multiple teams and helped many organizations across the country gain a competitive advantage through building a strong organizational culture. He is founder of The Center for Company Culture, a management consulting firm specializing in organizational culture and team development. He is also the architect of *The 4 C's Model to Creating a High-Performing Company Culture*. Tim's practical, simple, and straightforward approach has helped leaders and organizations tackle some of their biggest challenges, including employee engagement, leadership, teamwork, and more.

Tim lives in the Houston area with his wife and five children.

Made in United States
Orlando, FL
10 April 2022

16670238R10067